JEVINGTON, WANNOCK ~ AND ~ WILLINGDON

A Portrait in Old Picture Postcards and Photographs

Rosalind Hodge

S.B. Publications

For my Family

First published in 2003 by S. B. Publications,
19 Grove Road, Seaford, East Sussex BN25 1TP
Tel: 01323 893498

ISBN 1-85770-284-0

Designed and Typeset by EH Graphics (01273) 515527

ACKNOWLEDGEMENTS

I would like to thank the following for generously providing information:

Joan Barras, Sheila Dawson, Vera Hodsoll, Pam Linnett, Rice Medhurst, Ken Parris, William Pratt, Valerie Wardlow, James Wooller, Jenny Wootton.

Acknowledgements for permission to reproduce photographs:

Marion Hales: Rev Owen Tudor, Willingdon School Cricket Team. Vera Hodsoll: Wannock Farm, Wannock Watermill, Lower Mill. Mary Howard: Willingdon Pound. Pam Linnett: Hockington, Willingdon Pump, Ratton Staff. Olive Morgan: Willingdon School Stoolball Team. Ken Parris: Mr & Mrs Haylock, Willingdon Tea Rooms, Church Farm. Edward Reeves, Photographers of Lewes: 'Eight Bells'. William Still: Last Cart Boy. John Tyhurst: Staff Old Mill Gardens. Eastbourne Local History Society: Lord Willingdon. All others are from the author's collection.

Pictures: *Front Cover* - Red Lion, Willingdon
            Back Cover - Wannock Tea Gardens
                            School Hill, Jevington
            Title Page - Filching Manor

p.u. = postally used.

BIBLIOGRAPHY

Mills in Wannock Willingdon & Polegate - Vera Hodsoll (unpublished)

The Story of Wannock East Sussex - Mary Bruce-Wilson undated

Childhood Memories of Polegate Wind & Water Mills - Bertha Terry 1985

The Gardens at Wannock - Jennifer Wootton 1999

Memories of Old Willingdon - Harriet A Smith 1957

Old Willingdon - W J Vine 1978

History of Willingdon Golf Club 1898-1998 Phillip S Haffenden 1998

Place-Names of Sussex - English Place-Name Society Volume VII 1969

Domesday Book Sussex - John Morris 1976

Jevington Tithe Map & Award 1839

Willingdon Tithe Map & Award 1842

Gowlands Eastbourne Directories 1891-1914

Pikes's Eastbourne, Hailsham & District Blue Books 1890 -1934

Kelly's Directories of Sussex 1866-1970

Eastbourne Herald Chronicle

Eastbourne Gazette

Census Returns 1841, 1851, 1861, 1871, 1881, 1891, 1901

Jevington School Log 1873 - 1926

INTRODUCTION

Picture postcards, dating from the end of the 19th century, are reflections of a bygone age providing us with a valuable insight into our social and local history. Plain postcards appeared in 1870 but in 1894 the Post Office first issued licences for the production of picture postcards. These early cards, known as 'Court Cards', had one side for both the picture and writing.

In 1902, the British Post Office became the first to permit production of cards with divided backs, allowing correspondence, address and stamp on one side and the picture on the other. Postage was a $\frac{1}{2}$d inland and 1d abroad. Millions of cards were produced by thousands of long forgotten companies and individuals. Some local publishers included Carter & Co., Gowland Bros., Brooker & Son and FA Bourne.

Sending and collecting postcards became a national craze and most households boasted an album. This novel way of sending a message was used much as we use a telephone or email today. These prolific years, known as 'The Golden Age' lasted from 1902 - 1918, resulting in 800 million cards being sent in any one year in Edwardian Britain. The telephone and increased postage rates heralded the gradual decline of postcards.

However, twenty years ago interest was rekindled when dusty albums were discovered hidden in attics and cupboards, and today postcard collecting is enjoying a major revival.

This book of 105 vintage postcards and photographs takes the form of a nostalgic walk from the Downland village of Jevington, through the rural communities of Filching and Wannock to Willingdon. I hope it will rekindle happy memories for those who recall delightful days here when life was at a slower pace and also provide enjoyment for readers new to the area but with an interest in its past.

Rosalind Hodge, June 2003

JEVINGTON, WANNOCK AND WILLINGDON

The village of Jevington lies within a hollow of the South Downs approximately 4 miles North West of Eastbourne. Of the three areas it has changed the least, its somewhat isolated position cushioning it from modern development. It is a typical downland village with many of its 51 properties built of local flint. It is designated a Conservation Area with 22 listed buildings. The name Jevington is thought to originate from a Saxon leader who built a settlement here: GE(O)FA - leader, ING - people of, TON - a settlement. As with most place names its spelling has varied through the ages.

Until fifty years ago, Wannock at the northern end of Jevington parish was made up of a small cluster of cottages surrounding Wannock Farm, the Watermill and the Tea Gardens. Development began following the closure of the Old Mill Gardens and continued up to the 1970s with the sale of farmland and the Wannock Tea Gardens. The name Walnoch is recorded in 1086 and later Wannoc. Wann is Old English for stream, a possible reference to the Glen stream. From 1724 to 1873 it was called Walnut Street, no doubt due to the abundance of these trees in the area, some of which survive today.

The parish of Willingdon or Wilendone, as recorded in the Domesday Book, stands on a high spur at the foot of Combe Hill some 3 miles from the coast. Until boundary changes, in the last century, it reached from Hailsham to Westham taking in Hampden Park and Langney Point. Willingdon remained a rural community until the 1920s with a population of 884. The majority of land belonged to the Ratton Estate including twelve major and a number of smaller farms. Housing development began in the 1930s and continued rapidly after the war, changing the area drastically. By 1981 the population had risen to 5,896.

The civic parishes of Jevington and Willingdon were amalgamated in 1991.

JEVINGTON STREET P.U. 1907

This view of Jevington Street has changed little in the last century but socially things are very different. A hundred years ago the majority of villagers were employed on the land and in trades associated with farming. Jevington had a Wheelwright, Blacksmith and Farrier and social activities revolved around the Church, Village School and 'The Eight Bells'. There were also village shops and a Post Office. Electricity was brought to the village in 1932 but villagers had to rely on wells for water as there was no mains water until 1967.

HAWTHORNE LODGE, CYCLE REST C.1903

'Hawthorne Lodge' was built on the site of earlier cottages in 1865 by William Clay the famous jockey and racehorse trainer. From 1883 it was a Convalescent Home run by Mrs Emilie Crowe who trained with Florence Nightingale. By 1890 the Miller family had moved in and changed it to 'The Cyclists' Rest', serving teas and selling confectionery. Later still it was Mrs Armiger's village shop. Today you can still enjoy refreshment at 'Hawthorne Lodge' otherwise known as Jevington Tea Rooms.

THE HOMESTEAD c.1911

Part of this house, on the corner of Eastbourne Lane, dates from the 17th century. It has a fascinating history having been at various times, 'Swanky's Beer House', a butcher's, a general store and a bakery. Deeds show Elizabeth Rason ran a 'Coffee Chamber' here in 1730. Loftus Canton purchased and extensively altered and restored the property in 1910. Later it was owned by Rosa Lewis, friend of Edward VII, on whose life the BBC based the series, ' The Duchess of Duke Street'.

Jevington. Sussex II. 496.

DUMBRELL'S COTTAGES P.U. 1903

'Dumbrell's Cottages', opposite Church Lane, form a row of four cottages in two adjoining flint properties. In 1937 Mr Elliott, owner of a grocery store in South Street Eastbourne, bought and converted them to a single house. After the war Mr Newton-Blades turned this into a country hotel named 'The Monk's Rest'. In 1968 Nigel and Susan McKenzie bought the hotel and founded the 'Hungry Monk' restaurant where Banoffi Pie was first created. Opposite, Flint Cottages, originally named New Cottages, were built by the rector Edward Foley in 1873.

MRS FINCH'S TEA LAWNS P.U. 1903

Mrs Alice Finch, whose family lived in Jevington for several generations, ran a charming Tea Gardens at Dumbrell's Cottage on the corner of Willingdon Lane. It is reputed that, whilst on a visit to Compton Place, HRH Princess Mary visited the cottage with her governess and enjoyed tea in the garden. Mrs Finch is pictured here seated, with her cat on her lap, beside Alfreda her daughter.

JEVINGTON CHURCH C.1915

Walkers on the South Downs Way pass close by the ancient church of St Andrew's Jevington. The Saxon Tower c. 900AD is typical of a defensive tower built not only as a place of worship but as protection against the Vikings who landed at Cuckmere Haven and raided the coastal villages. Built of flint and local green sandstone it includes every style of medieval architecture. Roman tiles are visible in the North and South walls of the tower. A Saxon sculpture of Christ was found under the tower floor in 1785.

HARVESTING IN MONASTERY FIELD C.1913

The Village School closed for Harvest-time when men, boys and horses spent long days in the Jevington fields. Here Blaise, Brandy and Trooper pull the reaper and binder to harvest the corn in Monastery Field beside the church. The field derives its name from a Chapel dedicated to St. Lewinna, foundations of which were found here. Records show that in 1238 William de Montecute, Lord of the Manor, granted Jevington Chapelry to nearby Michelham Priory.

JEVINGTON RECTORY c.1914

This Queen Anne building was enlarged and much improved in 1873. It has chalk lined cellars which, in the 1950s, still showed the broad arrow marks left by the Excise men two hundred years before. There is little doubt that these cellars were used by smugglers in the 18th century and there are stories of a secret underground passage connecting the Rectory to nearby cottages. For 250 years it was home to the rectors of Jevington. In 1977 it was sold by the Chichester Diocese and is now a private house.

St. Aubyn's, Willingdon Lane c.1914

William Clay, the famous jockey and racehorse trainer, moved to Jevington in 1862. He built extensive stabling and this large family home in Willingdon Lane. He named the house 'St Aubyns', after a celebrated horse he had ridden to victory. Today the tradition of racehorse training in Jevington, which he started and continued for 40 years, still flourishes in the village.

WILLINGDON LANE P.U. 1911

Willingdon Lane, as the name suggests, forms the beginning of the track that leads over the Downs from Jevington to Willingdon. This attractive lane with its cluster of pretty cottages features in a drawing of 1750, part of the Burrell Collection in The British Library, by the famous 18th century artist Samuel Hieronymous Grimm. The 1881 census records 13 properties and 64 people living in the lane.

JEVINGTON SCHOOL BAND c.1879

Thomas Dimmer, Jevington schoolmaster from 1873-1882, formed a Fife and Drum band in 1877. He is pictured here with the schoolboys smartly dressed in their scarlet and black uniforms. Each wore a red sash and a peaked hat topped with a scarlet rosette and button. Twice a week, to the delight of villagers, Mr Dimmer marched the band four abreast up and down the main street. The boys were successful in winning several local competitions.

JEVINGTON SCHOOL P.U. 1908

On 31st December 1846 William Cavendish, Earl of Burlington, conveyed Link Field to the Rector and Churchwardens as a site for a school and school house. Before this children were taught in the church tower. The new National School, built high on a bank beside the main street, opened on 6th June 1847. In 1873 it was enlarged to accommodate 80 children from Wannock, Filching and Jevington. By 1926 there were too few pupils and it was closed by the Minister of Education. It was later used as the Post Office and is now the Village Hall.

MAY DAY, JEVINGTON SCHOOL c.1923

Each year for the May Day celebrations the school children made flower garlands and delighted villagers watched the traditional crowning of the May Queen and Maypole dancing. This charming postcard shows the whole school with May Queen Christobel Cuthbert sitting on her flower decked throne and Betty (Kath) Boniface holding her train. Schoolmistress, Edith Newson, wrote on this card that her 3 year old son Robert is seated centre front. Jevington School closed 7th January 1927 and pupils transferred to Willingdon Church School.

MEMORIAL CROSS 1900

Thomas Reuben Whittington was born at Wannock in 1886 and attended Jevington School. Aged 14 he was employed by J Wood & Son of Brook Street, Polegate. On 22nd October 1900 whilst placing a drag brake under the wheels of a cart loaded with flints it slipped killing him instantly. His body was taken to the 'Eight Bells' where an inquest was held. This cross set in the wall at 'Thorpe Cottages', now 'King's Farthing', marks the place of the accident.

ROAD MENDER C.1908

Mr Cox was the parish road man. Roads were constructed of clay and flints, becoming dry and dusty in summer but very muddy and sometimes almost impassable in wet weather. The road from Wannock to Filching Lime Kilns was particularly bad in winter with deep ruts caused by the coal arriving and the lime being taken to Polegate Station. Flints were collected from the surrounding fields, broken and graded, for filling pot holes and repairing the surface.

DEVONSHIRE HOUSE P.U. 1914

Alterations in 1924 revealed the original medieval manor house still forming the central portion of the building. For most of its history it has been known as Jevington Place and owned by many influential families including the Dukes of Devonshire. In 1896 the Duke sold it to Charles Wood who established a stud farm and re-named it 'Devonshire House'. Zorzis Michalinos bought the Stud in 1920 and changed the named back to 'Jevington Place'. It is now a working farm.

THORPE COTTAGES c.1912

These three old cottages, opposite the 'Eight Bells', were once known as 'Bank Cottages' and 'High House'. A tunnel, used by smugglers, ran from its cellars to the 'Eight Bells'. In 1910 Captain Canton bought and restored them raising the outer flint walls and replacing the thatch with tiles. At that time Samuel Thorpe had lived there all his life so the cottages were re-named after this old Jevington family. Mrs Irene Rainey later ran a small private school here. In the 1960s it was again restored and re-named 'Kings Farthing'.

THE EIGHT BELLS C.1925

Deeds dating from 1747 show this was a private house until 1800 when John Kine was the first victualler. The name 'Eight Bells' is first recorded in 1810 when Seaford Brewer John Gorring purchased it for £640. A tunnel running from the cellars to Thorpe Cottages was blocked up in 1956. In 1889 The Star Brewery, Eastbourne, bought the inn and later still it was acquired by Courage & Barclay who extended the premises in 1969. It is now a popular Free House.

JEVINGTON THE EIGHT BELLS TEA LAWNS.

THE EIGHT BELLS TEA LAWNS c.1920

The 'Eight Bells' was once as famous for tea as beer, with gardens and gazebos where cars now park. A Tea and Dance Hall, demolished in the 1980s, was very popular and Mrs Edith Bowdler, landlady for over 20 years, was renowned for her excellent cooking in the 1920s & '30s. Productions by a flourishing Jevington Drama Society were held in the old tea and dance hall, until 1971, on a unique stage constructed from Star Brewery beer crates.

JEVINGTON STREET, STREET FARM C.1929

Street Farm, at the northern end of the village, possibly derives its name from the Roman Street which crossed here. In the Tithe map of 1839 it is named 'Homestead', being situated on land called Homelands. The large flint barn beside the house was demolished in the late 1960s but the flint cart shed on the left has now been converted into an attractive house called 'Barn Cottage'. In the foreground is one of the three village ponds. This one has now dried up but one remains at Oxendean and the other in Green Lane is currently being restored.

OLD POST OFFICE P.U. 1906

These cottages at the northern end of Jevington, opposite Green Lane, were originally home to the village blacksmith and wheelwright before becoming the village post office. In 1878 letters arrived from Hawkhurst at 7.15am and were dispatched by the blacksmith at 6.55pm. By 1899 the post was delivered and collected twice a day from Polegate and there were also facilities for Parcel Post, Money Orders and Telegraphs. John Henty, the former Postmaster, is seen here drawing water from the well.

JOHN HENTY, JEVINGTON POSTMAN
c.1898

The Henty family were blacksmiths in Jevington for many years and still have a forge in Old Town, Eastbourne. In 1878 John Thomas Henty was the first recorded Letter Receiver for Jevington and delivered post to Wannock, Jevington and Friston until 1905. His daughter Mary Ann took over as sub-postmistress in 1899. She often hid money and money orders in a bolster, for safety, which caused problems when she died in 1931. Following her death, the Post Office was transferred to the Old School.

JEVINGTON VILLAGE.

933.

LINBURY P.U. 1913

These old flint cottages are on the corner of Green Lane, opposite the Old Post Office. George Meek lived here in the 1870s with his grandparents and describes the cottage in his fascinating autobiography 'George Meek Bath Chair-man'. In the 1950s the far cottage became derelict and was converted for garaging a horse-box for Jevington Stud. In 1991 the building was restored to a single house and re-named 'Water End'.

HILLSIDE COTTAGES c.1916

In 1729 two cottages were built on the corner of Green Lane and a further two added at the rear in 1792. From 1796 to 1837 it was 'The Farrier's Arms' with John Kine the first licensee. It was an ideal position for an inn being situated at the junction of the Friston to Wannock Road and the Eastbourne to Brighton coach road. Green Lane was the section of the coach road linking Jevington to Folkington. Threatened with demolition in 1959 the cottages were restored and re-named 'Coopers' and' Hillside Cottage'.

ASH FARM AND LIMEKILNS P.U. 1923

In 1837 lime kilns were built to burn chalk from the extensive surrounding quarries at Filching. 'The Ashe', named after land of the family de Asche (1285), was built in 1842 by John Davies Gilbert of East Dean. Ash Farm with the kilns had many tenants until the Barker family bought it in 1918. From 1935 until 1946 it became Jevington Youth Hostel and following this it reverted again to a private residence. Chalk is no longer quarried here.

FILCHING MANOR P.U. 1906

This 15th century Wealden Hall House with its central hall, solar and minstrel gallery has smoke-blackened roof timbers indicating there was once a hearth in the centre of the hall floor. A smuggler's passage runs from its cellars to the nearby Glen. By the 1800s it was divided into three farm tenements known as Filching Cottages and steadily became more dilapidated. From 1910-1912 it was restored and extended by John D Clarke for Loftus Canton who re-named it Filching Manor. Today the grounds house a Motor Museum which is open to the public.

Loftus H. Canton c.1910

Captain Loftus Henry Canton, son of Charles and Agnes, was born 31 August 1876 at Regents Park. Like his father he become a dental surgeon. From 1903 he lived at 'Pentlow', St Leonard's Road, Eastbourne and particularly enjoyed walking over the Downs. In 1910, he bought the 'Homestead', 'Ellen Cottage', now known as Jiggs, 'The Tithe Barn', 'Thorpe Cottage' and 'Filching Cottages'. All these properties in Jevington parish he had extensively altered, restored and conserved. He made his home at Filching Manor following the restoration of the medieval timber framed house.

GIBBY'S TEA COTTAGE P.U. 1932

Gibby's Cottage was built in the early 1920s on land that was part of Ash Farm. Originally named New Farm, Mrs Snell ran a smallholding here keeping a cow, goats, pigs, chickens and ducks. Thomas and Isabel Gibbons, hoteliers from Eastbourne, bought New Farm and opened it as Tea Rooms, naming it after their daughter May, whose nickname was Gibby. During World War II it was a favourite place with pilots from Friston Airfield. Today you can still enjoy good food in the pretty surroundings of Gibby's Cottage.

LOCAL BUS SERVICE c.1926

In 1926, the first return bus service ran twice daily from Jevington to Eastbourne. When Jevington School closed, Henry Twine from Polegate transported the Jevington children to Willingdon School in his yellow bus. Wannock Glen with its tea dances was a popular attraction on the Jevington Road and here the motor bus is waiting for passengers outside Dumbrell's Cottages.

WANNOCK GLEN ENTRANCE C.1924

From Victorian times, Wannock Glen was a popular beauty spot with shady walks and rustic bridges over the stream which fed Wannock Watermill. After World War I it was further developed when a tea pavilion was built across the stream attracting many visitors in charabancs. It was described in guide books as "A beauty spot and rendezvous for tea and dancing". The main entrance was almost opposite Filching Manor.

WANNOCK GLEN:- ON THE LAKE

WANNOCK TEA PAVILION P.U. 1923

There was a much greater volume of water in the Glen than today for two reasons. Firstly, there was the dam down stream necessary to create the mill pond and more recently the Water Company has extracted water from the stream. When the wooden pavilion was built further dams were constructed forming small lakes where visitors could hire punts and rowing boats. The pavilion and the balcony are seen here together with one of the boats.

WANNOCK GLEN: THE DANCE & TEA HALL.

WANNOCK GLEN DANCE AND TEAL HALL P.U. 1921

This postcard shows the interior of the pavilion with tables, piano and Chinese lanterns. It was supported on wooden stilts and was reputedly an old Army hut, possibly from Summerdown Camp, Eastbourne. There were wide doors which opened onto large balconies overlooking the water. Tea Dances with live music were a popular feature of the 1920s. Sadly, the venture only survived until 1930 when the owner was declared bankrupt. Today a section of the dam wall is the only part to survive.

WANNOCK MANOR FARM
c.1920

Parts of Wannock Manor Farmhouse date from the 16th century. During renovation, about thirty years ago, a lump of chalk found built into a wall had the inscription R Wood 1571. The house incorporates Elizabethan bricks and there are traces of holes cut in a beam for window bars, used before the days of glazing. In 1968 the farmhouse and 5 acres was sold and part of the land developed as Filching Close. The farmhouse was then re-named Wannock Place.

Last Cart Boy at Wannock Farm 1946

William Still was the last cart boy to be employed by Kenneth Marchant at Wannock Farm. This picture shows William with Alfred Hylands who lived at Broad Water Cottages, Wannock. They are bringing a cartload of rushes from Pevensey Marshes back to Wannock Farm where it was used as winter bedding for the livestock.

OLD THATCHED COTTAGE, WANNOCK C.1910

The Thatched Cottage was a typical example of an early 16th century Yeoman's Hall, thought by some archaeologists to date from earlier Feudal times. It was divided into two cottages before being bought by Mrs Lean and restored in 1910 by John D Clarke. On 20th February 1937 a disastrous fire, starting in the roof beside the chimney, reduced it to a shell as locals gathered to watch the ferocious blaze. Fortunately much of the valuable ancient timber was saved and it was re-built under the direction of architect John D Clarke.

THE HOMESTEAD TEA GARDENS c.1924

In the 1920s and 30s Mr & Mrs Richard Knight ran Tea Gardens here. This is somewhat surprising considering it was next-door to the Wannock Tea Gardens and opposite the Old Mill Gardens. Mrs Knight was well known for her homemade sweets which she sold from one of the green painted open-fronted summer houses in the garden. Honeywell Close now occupies the site where the Homestead once stood surrounded by its pretty cottage garden.

WANNOCK P.U. 1904

Wannock Strawberry Gardens, dating from around 1860, is situated behind the familiar grass triangle at the junction of Wannock Lane and Jevington Road. In 1904, the date of this postcard, Frederick Thomas occupied the cottage with his wife Kate. Over the years he specialised in fruit growing but developed the nursery, glass houses, gardens and tea lawns that were to become the famous Wannock Tea Gardens. Pillar Box Cottages are seen at the right of the picture.

Wannock from Tea Gardens

F.A. BOURNE, EASTBOURNE

VIEW DOWN THE WANNOCK ROAD TO POLEGATE C.1920

From the steps of Wannock Fruit & Tea Gardens, the road curves in the direction of Polegate. On the right are Stream Cottages and beyond on the left Old Mill Lane, Ivy and Willowbrook Cottages. The house visible on the left, with the double gables, was used as Whichello's Estate Office during the development of Cornmill Gardens in the mid 1960s. It was later demolished to make way for three bungalows.

THE SHOP
118 WANNOCK GARDENS, POLEGATE, Sx.

JAMES M. GREGG IN THE SHOP C.1918

James Gregg purchased the Gardens from the Thomas family around 1906 moving into the cottage with his wife. He continued to grow flowers and fruit in his gardens and glasshouses and here we see melons, grapes, apples and peaches displayed for sale. He often served in the little shop, which stocked home-made preserves, honey, Rowntree's, Havingden's and St George's Chocolates and of course picture postcards .

TEA LAWN, WANNOCK GARDENS C.1910

At the rear of the cottage the tea lawns were laid out with pretty flower beds, hanging baskets and also summerhouses and arbours in case the weather was less than perfect. Neatly dressed waitresses served the speciality of freshly picked strawberries, from the garden, with cream from Wannock Farm. Bread and cakes were brought over from the Old Mill Bakery so it is little wonder that visitors came from near and far to enjoy these treats in picturesque surroundings.

WANNOCK STRAWBERRY BEDS C.1919

In the 1860s Hopkins 'Guide to East-bourn and its Environs' describes the joys of picking your own strawberries at Wannock and eating them with cream and sugar. In its early days Wannock Gardens was known as the Strawberry Gardens, the original cottage being surrounded by fruit trees and soft fruit beds. It was such a popular attraction in the season that one can easily see how it grew and developed into the famous Tea Gardens. Later strawberries were grown under glass when these beds became part of the ornamental flower gardens.

In the image, handwritten text reads:

MOTOR PARK
TO ACCOMODATE 40 CHAR-A-BANCS
WANNOCK GARDENS
POLEGATE, Sx 121

WANNOCK MOTOR PARK c.1918

This card boasts accommodation for 40 Char-a-bancs. Chapman and Southdown were two of the companies who regularly brought visitors here. 'The Bungalow', a corrugated iron hut from the 1914-18 Polegate Royal Naval Air Station, was home to attendant Mr Tully and his family. Wannock Lane is to the left of the picture and on the horizon the spire of Willingdon church is just visible between the trees.

WOOTTON'S WANNOCK GARDENS *c.*1927 WANNOCK *near Eastbourne* CAR PARK *with* ATTENDANT

WOOTTON'S WANNOCK GARDENS C.1927

Twenty years after buying the Wannock Gardens, James Gregg decided to retire. The house and gardens were bought by Walter Wootton in June 1926 who, seeing their potential, immediately planned to expand and improve them. Walter, an experienced caterer, was a great believer in advertising and above is the cover of a booklet produced shortly after his arrival. Here he advertises increased space for 250 cars and even aeroplane flights providing aerial views over the Gardens, Glen and Downs.

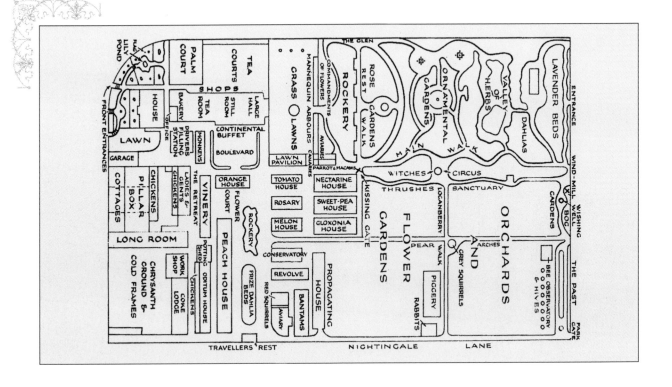

WANNOCK GARDENS PLAN c.1928

This plan from the original booklet shows the lay-out of the gardens. Running down the left hand side of the plan is the Jevington Road and Wannock Lane runs across the top. Beyond the right hand edge is the car park and nurseries where many varieties of fruit and flowers were grown. It is worth noting that the orchard, in the lower right-hand corner, was later the site of Slaymaker's Model Village.

Palm Court Woottons Wannock Gardens, Polegate, Sussex.

PALM COURT c.1930

In 1915 James Gregg built a large tea room, to the left of the house, known as the Palm Court. This provided comfortable indoor seating and much of the glass incorporated in the building came from Boots the Chemist in Eastbourne which was being rebuilt at the time. The Palm House was a well-known feature of the Wannock Tea Gardens until it finally closed on Sunday 29th September 1969.

1555. LARGEST HALL, WOOTTONS, WANNOCK GARDENS.

LARGEST TEA HALL c.1927

On 18 May 1927 the Deputy Mayor of Eastbourne, Councillor Knight, opened Walter Wootton's new tea hall. Those who remember the gardens will recall it above the shop, kitchen and still room areas. It provided seating for over 400 and was used for dances, whist drives and as a badminton court. During World War II Canadian troops were billeted in the tea room and the gardens were turned over to food production.

TEA COURTS, WOOTTON'S WANNOCK GARDENS

TEA COURTS C.1930

From the Tea Courts the rear of the Palm Court is visible in the background and the chimney of the house. Along the left side of the photo is the shop, kitchens and still room with the large tea hall and its surrounding balcony above. To the right is the boundary with Wannock Lane. These courts are in the same position as the original tea lawns of the Wannock Fruit & Tea Gardens, as pictured earlier, in the days of Frederick Thomas and James Gregg.

Prize Dahlia Growing Woottons Wannock Gardens, Polegate, Sussex

THE GARDENS AND GLASS HOUSE C.1930

Walter Wootton's son Harold was trained in horticulture and his skills soon became evident in the gardens. He re-designed the layout creating new pathways and flower beds. Local builder Albert Fielder and his workmen did much of the work and also built the new cacti, orchid and tropical houses. Surrounding this dahlia bed are glasshouses where melons, peaches, oranges, lemons, pineapples and bananas flourished. Strawberries were still grown for sale in the shop and for strawberry teas.

MODEL VILLAGE C.1953

Fred Slaymaker's hobby of model making grew over the years into Slaymaker's Wonder Village. From 1953 it was a well-loved part of Wannock Gardens where it occupied the area of the former Bee Observatory. Fred and his wife moved from West Sussex to Broad Road and here, each winter, he created new models for his village. These included the church, castle, tavern, shops and cottages but everyone's favourite was the colourful working fairground with revolving gallopers, swing boats and big wheel.

BIRDS PARADISE LEADING TO VALLEY OF HERBS, WOOTTON'S WANNOCK GARDENS.

BIRD'S PARADISE C.1930

From the Rockery and Rose Garden white fan-tailed doves fluttered around the dovecote in Bird's Paradise pictured here. This led into the Valley of Herbs with a profusion of lavender bushes and other sweetly scented plants. Wannock Lavender, Pot-Pourri and Rosemary Bags were a favourite souvenir of the gardens. In 1928 prices for these ranged from 8d to 3/6d and were available by mail order, postage free on orders over 15 shillings..

MAIN WALK, WOOTTON'S WANNOCK GARDENS.

WITCHES' CIRCUS C.1950

Just off the Main Walk was the Witches' Circus. Mirrored glass Witches' Balls, manufactured in various colours, were popular objects in Edwardian times. The silver mirrored ball was mounted on a stone pedestal beneath an arbour of climbing roses, clematis and honeysuckle. A peep into the magic glass ball was said to give a glimpse into the future and was a perennial attraction with the numerous visitors to the gardens.

VIEW TOWARDS WANNOCK WATER MILL P.U. 1903

This view from the bend at Wannock Road shows the Mill House and the Mill to its left. George Thomas who lived here also owned Willingdon Windmill and the lower Watermill. Three large glasshouses were cultivated by George's son Charles and two of these were later to become the Japanese and the Winter Gardens. Frederick, George's eldest son, lived at the Wannock Fruit & Tea Gardens across the road. These two brothers created the Old Mill Gardens from 1906.

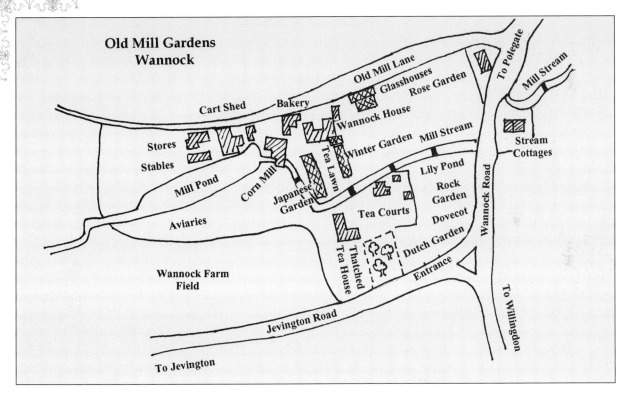

MAP OF OLD MILL GARDENS c.1920

The Garden's entrance was approximately where the entrance to Mill Close is today. The western section of Old Mill Lane is built on the site of the mill pond and the Twitten from Jevington Road to Old Mill Lane follows the boundary between the Gardens and Wannock Farm's field. The path crosses the stream near the site of the Japanese Garden. The Corn Mill would have been on your left and the Bakery stood between the Mill and Wannock House.

WANNOCK WATER MILL C.1890

It is not known when a mill first existed at Wannock but a map dated 1620 clearly shows the mill and pond. Having worked for over 300 years, it ceased to grind corn shortly after 1917. By 1956 it had fallen into such disrepair that it was demolished. The mill pond was filled in and bungalows built on the site. All trace of it has now disappeared except for the name Old Mill Lane and the narrow stream flowing between the modern properties.

MAID OF THE MILL C.1920

This carved wooden figure hung above the mill door is thought to be Jacobean. It represents the miller's wife holding a measure and strike, illustrating the custom of payment in kind. When poor folk brought grain to be ground but couldn't afford to pay, a measure of one gallon from each bushel was taken as payment. A member of the Turner family, who were the last bakers at the Old Mill, still owns this fascinating figure.

OLD MILL BAKERY c.1920

These carts standing in front of the cart shed and granary are ready to set off on deliveries from Wilmington to Eastbourne. Katie Thomas, one of the daughters, had painted poppies, wheat and 'Thomas's Country Bread' on the second cart from the right. In 1917 the Bakery was taken over by H E Turner who owned a bakery in Polegate and he then supplied all the bread and cakes to the gardens. The Turners ran Wannock Bakery until its closure in 1955 when their business moved to Victoria Drive, Eastbourne.

WANNOCK HOUSE, OLD MILL GARDENS P.U. 1920

In 1826 Henry Thomas came to Wannock as apprentice miller to Joseph Seymour and married his daughter Phyllis. In 1906/7 their grandsons, Charles and Frederick, started the Old Mill Tea Gardens at Wannock House. In 1912 Charles married florist Ethel Gladding and her father Walter joined the partnership which lasted until 1930 when the house and gardens were sold to Alfred J Frazer. He ran it as a guesthouse for two years before selling to Walter Wootton. Ethel Thomas is seen here seated beside waitress Annie Ticehurst.

OLD MILL GARDENS, WANNOCK: THE TEA COURT.

TEA COURTS C.1920

The Tea Courts were situated on the opposite side of the stream to the main house and were reached by way of one of the pretty rustic bridges. Two large thatched tea pavilions provided shade and shelter among the colourful flower beds. It was not unusual to have the company of peacocks which strutted about the gardens. Ornamental trees, including old mulberry and walnut trees, surrounded the stone paved courts creating a picturesque sheltered sun-trap.

STAFF OF THE OLD MILL GARDENS C.1934

This photograph shows some of the staff of the Old Mill Gardens at a party in July 1934. Mabel Ovenden was the cook and Annie Ticehurst, seated front right, was the head waitress for many years. Others who worked there were: Mrs Hylands, Mrs Hastings, Miss Annie Smith, Miss Bradford and Mrs Emily Wooller. In 1926 Annie Smith wrote a long descriptive poem about the Gardens and later copies were printed and sold as popular souvenirs.

ROCK GARDEN AND LILY POND P.U. 1920

Charles Thomas was a trained horticulturalist and together with Frederick, his brother, they laid out beautiful gardens around the mill and house incorporating the natural beauty of the stream. Paths wound through formal gardens, rustic bridges crossed the stream and pretty thatched gazebos provided shady corners in which to sit and enjoy the delightful vistas. Stream Cottages in Wannock Road can be seen back left.

JAPANESE GARDEN c.1925

About 1895 some farm buildings surrounding Wannock House were demolished and replaced with three large glasshouses. Charles Thomas, younger son of the miller, grew fruit and flowers in these and also cultivated part of the land as orchards. When the Tea Gardens were developed Japanese Landscape Gardeners, T Yano & Co., created a wonderful garden in one of these glasshouses . It featured streams and fountains, bonsai trees and miniature bamboo interspersed with pagodas, bridges and temples.

WINTER GARDEN P.U. 1925

Another of the large glasshouses backed on to a conservatory at the rear of Wannock House. This was the Winter Garden where teas were served when the weather was cooler and a succession of plants provided colour and scent all year round. Jasmine, ivy and honeysuckle climbed up supports and palms provided a central focus of the floral displays. So, whatever the weather tea could be enjoyed in this attractive setting.

WANNOCK HOUSE GARDENS:- OLD RUSTIC BRIDGE.

RUSTIC BRIDGE P.U. 1921

The roof of the bakery is seen top right and behind this, to the left, the gable-end of the Watermill is just visible. There was a team of gardeners who tended the grounds and here William Putland, head gardener, is standing on the rustic bridge. This bridge led visitors across the mill stream to the aviaries housing exotic foreign birds and to the mill pond where swans glided gracefully on the still water.

DUTCH SUMMER HOUSE AND ROCKERY C.1919

A feature of the Dutch and Rock Garden was this pretty domed summer house made entirely of thatch. In spring the beds were ablaze with colourful bulbs, sweet scented stocks and forget-me-nots. These gave way to large flowered begonias and pots of blue agapanthus in the summer months. The lovely sundial depicted Atlas holding up the world. The roof of the cottage at Wannock Fruit & Tea Gardens is just visible through the trees.

WILLINGDON WINDMILL
P.U. 1923

This fine brick Tower Mill, standing 45 feet high, was built in Willingdon by Joseph Seymour, probably in 1817 the date inscribed on the mill. For 122 years it stood within the parish until the civil parish of Polegate was formed in 1939. Millers included Matthias Mockett and George Thomas of Wannock and from 1918 the Ovenden family. Eastbourne & District Preservation Trust bought the mill, from Albert Ovenden in 1965, saved and restored it. The Duke of Devonshire officially opened it to the public on 1st July 1967.

THE LOWER WATER MILL

Nothing remains of the Watermill, built in 1833 by Joseph Seymour. It stood 300 yards west of the windmill and together with Wannock Watermill, all had at one time been owned by the Seymour and Thomas families. Development of surrounding land brought risk of flooding and heralded the mill's demise and sale in 1972. It was demolished in 1974, the wheel going to Wateringbury mill. Albert Ovenden, the last miller, stands to the right of the picture. The Millrace cul-de-sac and flats now stand on the site.

ROYAL NAVAL AIR STATION C.1916

Polegate Royal Naval Air Station stood entirely within Willingdon Parish and was operational from 6th July 1915. The main entrance, shown here, was at the Triangle with Coppice Avenue and Broad Road following the original Air Station roads. Huge hangers housed six Sea Scout airships which patrolled The Channel from Dungeness to Portland Bill seeking out and attacking enemy vessels. After the war the buildings were auctioned off but two remained; one serving as Willingdon Library and another, until the mid 1990s, as Bird's Engineering works.

WILLINGDON A.R.P. WARDENS C.1944

Willingdon Wardens are pictured here from left to right. Seated: Mary Searle, F Hinsby, Tom Searle, Arthur Dodd, Leonard Tweedale, Mrs Wilson. 2nd row Sidney Wheeler, Mrs Wheeler, Daphne Pearce, Kitty Hopkins, Miss Burgess, Bill Harden, Harold Lockwood. 3rd row: George Rolfe, Fred Morgan, H Bishop, J Priest, 'unknown' , Fred Moore. Back row: Mr Heborn , Albert Fielder, longest serving senior warden in Hailsham Rural District, Fred Prodger, D Winder. The air raid warning and all-clear was 'phoned through from Eastbourne Police Station to Bird's Engineering Works where the siren was housed and manually operated.

The Parade, Lower Willingdon.

ORCHARD PARADE C.1936

This row of shops in Orchard Parade at The Triangle was built in 1935 by the local builder Albert E Fielder for W Lawrence a local butcher. During the 1914-18 war this area was included within the Royal Naval Airship Station. Before this, as the name suggests, it had been an orchard. Off the right of the picture was Willingdon Steam and Hand Laundry, now Brains the butchers. The Triangle was once Mr Manser's strawberry garden and later geese were kept here.

THE BRITISH QUEEN C.1920

The 'B. Q.' as it is fondly known was originally a double fronted Georgian building probably formerly two cottages. Customers entering the front door turned right into the Tap Room with its bare floorboards and hatch where the beer was served. Across the passage, on the left was the Beer Parlour. Today's mock Tudor facade was built in 1935 when the Star Brewery engaged Herbert Compton to re-design some of its houses, including the 'Wheatsheaf' in this attractive style. Courage Brewery took it over in 1965 and enlarged the property.

BARNSIDE TEA GARDENS C.1928

Until the late 1800s part of Wannock Lane was called Rapson's Lane. It led to Rapson's Farm and Barn at the junction with the present day Gorringe Valley Road. In 1925 Thomas Martin, a nurseryman, moved into a new bungalow beside the barn, named 'Barnside' and his wife opened Tea Gardens. 'TEAS' was painted in large white letters on the slate barn roof but the venture only lasted 5 years. Houses now stand on the site of 'Barnside' and Rapson's Barn is converted into a house.

WILLINGDON TEA ROOMS AND SHOP c.1907

Willingdon Tea Rooms and grocery shop was situated at Lower Willingdon where number 5 Southdown Cottages now stands. This photograph was taken before numbers 1, 2 & Southdown Cottages were built around 1908 and these existing cottages were altered a few years later. The main road, Red Lion Street, ran right in front of these houses and the path which led to the shop can still be seen between the present day houses. Beyond is the horse pond, now enclosed, and the British Queen.

Lower Willingdon 261.

ROSEBANK COTTAGES P.U. 1905

This row of 8 cottages called 'Rosebank' stood on the main Eastbourne Road between what is now Meachants Lane and Gorringe Valley Road. The old road is clearly visible winding round towards the Triangle in the distance. In 1905 this part of the Lewes Road was locally known as Red Lion Street. The new main road was built to the right of the picture, in 1934, bypassing the Triangle. The cottages were demolished in the mid-1960s to make way for 'Carmen Court'.

DANN'S FARM C.1887

The house, dating from the mid-16th century, was originally named Marshams. Jasper Dann lived here in 1725 and the farmland covered Combe Rise, Portsdown Way, Manor Close and part of Coopers Hill. In 1887 Emil Heinneman owned the property but he lived as tenant at Ratton Manor. John D Clarke the architect lived here in 1920. Miss Towers bought and changed the name to Portsdown Manor in 1926. Charles and Jane Wooller are pictured outside the front door of Dann's Farm with their children. Charles later became bailiff to Freeman Thomas at Ratton.

CHALK FARM P.U. 1949

This 17th century farmhouse, now an hotel, is thought to have been built on the site of an ancient priory. The farm was part of the Ratton Estate, and John Paxton was tenant from 1856. One of his three daughters married a young farmer Thomas Cooper who eventually took over Chalk Farm. Through the gate was a circular drive with central flower bed where the Bonfire Society finished the annual torch-light procession. The pet peacock named Raja was a favourite with the village children. The family name Cooper is remembered in Coopers Hill.

WILLINGDON C.1905

This photograph was taken from the area which is now Wedderburn Road. In the foreground stands Wayside House, the village paper shop, library and Spring Bakery. The large Georgian house, front right, was an ironmonger's shop selling paraffin, soap and garden tools. This belonged to Robert Russell as did the village forge which stood behind the shop in Spring Terrace. The large building to the left of St Mary's church steeple is The Hoo. The terraced gardens covered a large area where Hoo Gardens and Ruskin Road now stand.

CHURCH STREET, LOOKING WEST C.1902

The two thatched cottages on the right were demolished in 1904 to make way for new houses. On the left are four cottages, Queen Anne's Terrace, whose first floor front doors opened directly on to the street. Their rear gardens had been a former marl pit known as Battimer's Hole. Dick Martin's sweet shop, originally Timson's bakery, was between the terrace and the 'Wheatsheaf'. This was enlarged taking in Granny Lewis's cottage on the corner of Church and Red Lion Street. The shop and terrace were replaced with modern houses in 1967.

BETTRIDGE'S SHOP, CHURCH STREET c.1930

Bettridge brothers bought the village grocery and drapery shop in 1930 from Alfred Hutchings. Originally four cottages, the shop entrance was down a long garden path. Inside were two polished mahogany grocery counters and a marble one for butter and cheese. On the floor open sacks with pewter scoops held rice, tapioca, split peas and various dried fruits. Large black, red and gold canisters contained teas and coffee. A third counter held a whole range of ladies and gents wear from suits to working smocks and boots. It is now the house 'Old Place'.

CHURCH FARM HOUSE c.1890

Church Farm House is seen on the left and beyond is the entrance to Hutchings shop. Opposite stood the cattle yard, cart sheds and warehouse with a granary above. The farm house, later named 'St Wifred's', became the home of Alexander Wedderburn's housekeeper at 'The Hoo'. Church Farm then transferred to the eastern end of Church Street towards Jordons. When the estate was eventually sold the old farmhouse was re-named 'Combe House'. 'Marlowe' was built on the site of the cattle yard and buildings.

THE HOO P.U. 1910

The Saxon word 'Hoo', meaning ridge or spur, describes the site of this former Georgian farmhouse. When wealthy Scottish Q.C. Alexander Wedderburn bought the property in 1904 he employed the young Edwin Lutyens to re-design the house. Together with Gertrude Jekyll he designed beautiful terraces and gazebos leading down to lily ponds, glasshouses, orchards and kitchen gardens. For a while it was Clovelly Kepplestone Ladies College. In 1955 the house was divide into flats and the grounds sold for development. Ruskin Road is so named as Wedderburn edited his works.

Cottages opposite Church P.U. 1908

The two cottages on the right dating from 1758 are faced entirely with round boulders. They were originally a farmhouse with farmyard and orchard. In 1857 a row of flint cottages was built adjoining. The cottage featuring a distinctive Dutch-style gable was the Police Station complete with lock-up cell. Beyond, built on the old orchard, is 'Orchard' and 'Roma' now named 'Flags Rest'. Off the right of the picture is a building of square knapped flint part of an important house dating from 1611. In the 1800s it was used as a corn store.

WILLINGDON CHURCH P.U. 1908

Willingdon church, built of local flint and sandstone, was dedicated to St Mary the Virgin in 1946 and stands on the site of an earlier Norman church. The oldest parts of the present building, the inner porch door and tower, are 12th or early 13th century. The Medieval Ratton Chapel contains fine monuments to the Parker and Freeman-Thomas families and restored glass dating from 1622. The tower has six bells and the clock commemorates Queen Victoria's Golden Jubilee of 1877.

REV. OWEN TUDOR C.1902

Owen Lechmere Tudor M.A. is Willingdon's longest serving vicar. The son of a barrister, he was born 3 March 1854 at Kensington and attended Trinity College, Cambridge where he was a Cricket 'Blue'. He was curate of Christ Church, Eastbourne before coming to Willingdon where he served for 41 years from 1888-1929. Owen and Brenda, his wife, had four sons who attended Hydneye House School and one daughter. Owen was naturally a great supporter of the village cricket team. There is a plaque to his memory on the pulpit.

AUGUSTUS HAYLOCK C.1920

Augustus Alfred Haylock was born at Hanover Square, London in 1857. He studied at London University, entered the teaching profession and was appointed Headmaster of Willingdon Church School in 1881. Together with his wife Emma, who was Infant Mistress, they taught at the little school for 42 years. Augustus was the first organist at Willingdon church, a post he occupied for 28 years and was founder of the village band. They retired in 1923 moving to 'Bijou' in Church Street. A plaque to their memory is set in the wall by the church entrance.

WILLINGDON SCHOOL STOOLBALL TEAM c.1936

Willingdon School had a reputation for producing winning teams in the traditional Sussex game of Stoolball. The school won the County Championship for a number of years and here Mrs Christian and Mr Walter Wills, Headmaster, are pictured with the winning team of 1936. Standing from left to right: Edith Gay, Winifred Turner, Olive Penn, Lillian Wheatley, Dorothy Barker, Margery Willard, Marjorie Adams. Seated from left to right: Sheila Gurr, Josephine Tully, Gladys Brown, Joan Brown, Joan Fielder.

WILLINGDON SCHOOL CRICKET TEAM C.1932

The team is pictured in the playing field, at the rear of houses opposite the school in Church Street. The church tower is clearly visible above the roof tops. Standing from left to right: Len Humphrey, James Wooller, Fred Lawrence, Arthur Tugwell, Ronnie Catt, Ernie Manser, Arthur Wickins. Seated from left to right: Ken Walters, Ernest Cuthbert, Jack Hunnisett, Harold Ranger, Roy Hollobone. The names of Harold Ranger and Roy Hollobone are recorded on the War Memorial in Willingdon Church.

The Old Pound

OLD POUND, WILLINGDON P.U. 1912

The Village or Manor Pound in Church Street was used to impound stray cattle until claimed by their owners. It stood beside the school playground, by a field called Upper Hannty and the Parsonage Barn. The footpaths from Polegate, Lower Willingdon, Hampden Park and Ratton converged here with stone stiles on either side of the road. The house built beside the pound is named Pound Cottage. The 1934 Willingdon bypass bisected Church Street at this point and the old cattle pound disappeared under the tarmac.

HAYSTOUN HOUSE C.1930

This imposing Georgian house in Church Street, was originally named 'Shortlands'. In 1928 it was purchased by wealthy Major Aubrey Thorold du Plat Cole OBE, JP, MC and re-named 'Haystoun House'. He also purchased and demolished 'Hopedene School', adding its extensive grounds to the already spacious gardens of 'Haystoun House'. Major Cole was High Sheriff and Deputy Lieutenant of Sussex. Haystoun House is now divided into apartments and Haystoun Park and Bredon occupies the Hopedene site.

THE LODGE c.1918

Another fine Georgian house with spacious grounds once stood in Church Street on the site now occupied by Lodge Avenue, Shortlands Close and Wealden Park. Its original name was 'Buckingham Lodge' which was changed over the years to 'The Lodge' and finally 'White Lodge'. From 1907-1923 it was occupied by a family named Raleigh, descendants of Sir Walter Raleigh. In the 1950s Willingdon Church summer fetes were held in the grounds.

Hydneye House, Willingdon, Sussex.

Published from Photo by G. & R. Lavis, Eastbourne.

Oct. 2nd 1906

HYDNEYE HOUSE SCHOOL P.U. 1906

Hydneye House, in Church Street, was originally named 'The Lawn'. Boys from this Preparatory School were a common site in the village wearing red caps embroidered with silver letters HHS. Headmaster Leonard Norman and his wife Hope changed the name to 'Hopedene' around 1920. P J Ellis bought the school and built himself a house named 'Bredon' in the grounds. In 1932 the school moved to larger premises in Battle and 'Hopedene' was bought and demolished by Major Cole. The village stocks once stood on the bank just beyond here.

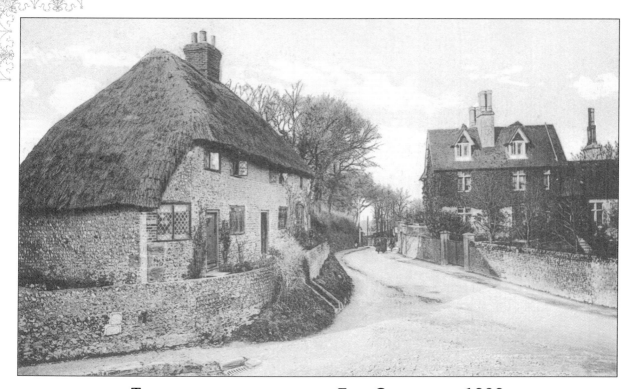

Thatched cottage and the Five Gables p.u. 1908

'Briar Cottage' and 'Rose Cottage' on the north west corner of Butts Lane were the last thatched properties in this part of the village, surviving until they were demolished in the 1960s. Tommy Stevens ran his carrier's business from 'Rose Cottage' and is pictured with his horse and trap on the front cover of this book. Opposite is 'Flint House', later re-named 'The Five Gables'. Beside this was originally a farmyard. The present day 'Wheatsheaf' car park, in Church Street, was originally the stables and coach house of 'Flint House'.

MALTHOUSE AND COTTAGES P.U. 1904

The ivy clad Malthouse was once a thatched farmhouse and reputedly the village beadle's residence. In the 1880s Lord Willingdon converted part of the house into a Reading Room. In Malthouse Cottages, to the left, a blocked up door for lifting in grain can still be seen. One cottage was the original Post Office and the position of the letterbox is still visible. As the coach passed each morning the mail sack was thrown from the top window. Mail was delivered in the morning but villagers had to collect their own post in the afternoon.

WILLINGDON POST OFFICE P.U. 1906

The 16th century building, on the right, was originally a Bakery and Tea-room. From 1906 the baker was also Sub-Postmaster and today it is still the Post Office. The bake-house and stabling for a pony and cart was at the rear, down 'Little Lane' twitten. Beside the Post Office is French's Yard and thatched Pelham Cottage. Mr Potter closed the bakery in 1940 but his wife continued as the popular postmistress. The lime tree on the forecourt commemorating Queen Victoria's 1862 Silver Jubilee was replaced with an Acer in 1977 marking Elizabeth II's Silver Jubilee.

RED LION c.1903

The old Red Lion, on the left, was an inn and coaching stop before 1787. It was rebuilt in 1907 in the half timbered style we see today and cottages stood on what is now the car park. At the rear was stabling and a large wash and mangle room where the women brought their washing for one penny and no doubt caught up with village gossip. Above this was a long room used for meetings and the annual Christmas Ball. Behind this was the Platt where the men played quoits after quenching their thirsts.

Hockington R.24
WILLINGDON

WILLINGDON LAVENDER GARDENS P.U. 1918

In 1908 Frederick and Mary Ann Morgan moved to Hockington House, the Tea & Lavender Gardens, with their 7 children. Pictured here from the lavender beds, much of the land was given over to a nursery and twice weekly Fred delivered produce in his horse and cart. During World War I they accommodated officers from Polegate Airship Station. For 26 years the family ran the gardens where sons, Walter (Mac), Luther, Fred, and Lindsay (Bub) worked in the nursery and daughters, Olive, Grace and Winnie helped with the teas.

VILLAGE PUMP HOUSE C.1910

The Village Pump House was built in 1880 by William Broderick Thomas and his initials and the date were set in the original gable. Constructed from flint with panels of sheep's knuckle bones it stands over the site of an ancient dipping hole and later well. The chalk stream emerging from the Downs crossed the fields, now Upper Kings Drive, where watercress once grew in abundance. It then continues to Hampden Park. It was the main source of drinking and domestic water apart from some deep wells in the village.

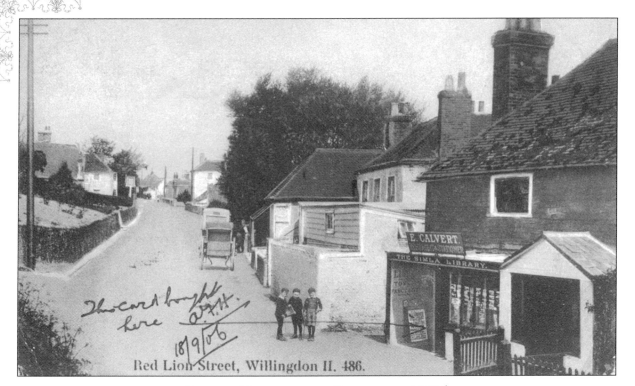

Red Lion Street, Willingdon II. 486.

SPRING BAKERY AND SHOP P.U. 1906

Spring Bakery, named after the spring feeding the village pump, stood on the site now occupied by 'Dorchester Court'. It was established in 1875 by Alfred Timson, a fancy bread and biscuit maker, tea dealer and confectioner formerly of Church Street. The Venner family ran it from 1914 until 1957. Next-door Calvert's sold newspapers, tobacco, sweets and local postcards. It also housed the Simla Lending Library. So when Mr West took over the shop in 1922 it was known simply as 'The Library', Red Lion Street. Today it is the Library hairdressing salon.

RATTON FARM c.1908

Ratton Farmhouse was built on the site of the original Medieval Manor House. The land covered Ratton Bottom from Wish Hill to Babylon Plantation including the dew pond and the Combe. It supplied eggs, milk, cheese and meat to the house. Following the sale of the Estate the farm buildings were converted into houses and now form part of the attractive development called Ratton Village. The bell, housed in a small tower in the stable yard, rang out every day at 12 noon and 5pm and still remains intact.

LORD WILLINGDON C.1926

Freeman Thomas was born 12th September 1866 at Ratton, baptised at Willingdon Church and in 1892 he married Marie Adelaide, daughter of Earl Brassey. From 1900 he was firstly M.P for Hastings then became Governor of Bombay and Madras, Governor General of Canada and Viceroy of India. When created Baron Willingdon in 1910 he changed his name to Freeman Freeman-Thomas. In 1936 he became Warden of the Cinque Ports and was created 1st Marquis of Willingdon. He died at Pimlico in August 1941 and is buried in Westminster Abbey.

Ratton Manor p.u. 1905

The Manor of RADETONE is recorded in the Domesday Book. This Tudor style Manor House was built 1899-1901 following a fire which gutted the earlier Georgian house. Surrounded by wonderful gardens there were magnificent views from the terraces to the sea. Ratton was Lord Willingdon's home until 12th November 1918 when the Estate was sold in lots by Public Auction. It was badly damaged by fire in 1941 whilst occupied by Canadian Forces. After the war it was demolished by the Willingdon firm F J French and Sons and the land was developed in the 1950s and 60s.

RATTON ESTATE WORKERS c.1914

This photograph shows Ratton Estate workers and their families on the occasion of a party to celebrate the 21st birthday of Gerard Frederick Freeman-Thomas, elder son of Lord and Lady Willingdon. Gerard was killed on active service a few months later on 14th September 1914. His premature death precipitated the sale of Ratton Park Estate after the war. The title passed to his brother Inigo who died in 1979 without heirs..

VIEW FROM RATTON WILLINGDON

RATTON MANOR GARDENS c.1813

Lady Willingdon took particular interest in Ratton's beautiful gardens, reputedly the finest in the area. The Grove was surrounded by high clipped yew hedges and enclosed wonderful examples of topiary such as birds, pyramids and spirals. Across the drive was the Rose Walk with arbors of fragrant rambler roses and two flint-walled gardens. One was used for soft fruits and, in the second, peaches and pears were trained against the walls and exotic fruits grew in heated glasshouses.

PARK FARM P.U. 1903

The beautiful farmhouse with its duck pond was situated in Park Farm Lane which led directly to Ratton Manor. One of the larger farms on the Estate, the land of 'The Park' extended to the North of Decoy Drive and Woodlands Avenue. This land later became known as 'Spots Farm'. Following the disastrous fire at Ratton in 1891, the silver and valuables from the manor were stored by John Filder who lived at 'The Park'. It is now a private house re-named Old Manor House.

WESTLORDS P.U. 1917

Westlords, almost opposite the entrance gates to Ratton Manor, was built in 1906. It stands in what was originally the Manor's walled kitchen gardens. The high flint garden walls remain along the Eastbourne Road and the North side of Park Lane. The grounds of over 5 acres included the old village cricket pitch. During World War II it was requisitioned by the War Office for Canadian troops, some of which took part in the Dieppe raid. In 1950, the Electricity Board purchased it for £19,000 to use as their District Offices..

Willingdon Golf Links.

WILLINGDON GOLF CLUB BUS C.1911

In 1898 Peter Paxton designed a 9-hole golf course on Ratton Park Estate with Mr Freeman-Thomas as 1st President. In 1903 a new clubhouse and another 9 holes were added. The Club Bus was purchased in 1911 to transport members and guests from Eastbourne hotels and Hampden Park Station. Mr Clark drove, cleaned and maintained it for 30 shillings a week. Petrol rationing in 1916 and increasing private motoring prevented its survival beyond 1918. In 1925 Alexander MacKenzie re-modelled the course.

ABOUT THE AUTHOR

Rosalind Hodge was born in Willingdon where she and four generations of her family still live. Her ancestors are first recorded in Willingdon Church registers in 1643 and at Jevington in the early 1800s. They farmed in both villages and served as churchwardens and parish councillors. She loves the Downs, wildlife and old rural customs and crafts. In 1987 she appeared in ITV's 'Country Ways' and is pictured on the parish millennium map. Her love of local history grew from memories told and recorded by her grandparents. She has a collection of over 400 local postcards and photographs.